759.2 COO

BERYL COOK'S
NEW YORK

BERYL COOK'S
NEW YORK

JOHN MURRAY

© Beryl Cook 1985
First published 1985
by John Murray (Publishers) Ltd
50 Albemarle Street, London W1X 4BD

Printed in Italy by New Interlitho SpA
Origination by Anglia Reproductions
British Library CIP Data

Cook, Beryl
  Beryl Cook's New York.
  1. Cook, Beryl
  I. Title
  759.2   ND497.C723

ISBN 0-7195-4229-4

Preface

In 1983 I spent, with my husband John, just over three weeks in New York and these paintings are the record of our stay there. Since I started painting, about twenty years ago, most of the incidents that have amazed, amused or, occasionally, annoyed me have been painted up in due course. I like the everyday activities of ordinary people like myself – busy shopping, working, drinking and generally enjoying life. I would really like to be the one who gets up to sing a song in the bar, races through the streets on roller-skates, juggles with beer-bottles in the park or tap-dances on a street corner with an admiring circle around me. As I am far too inhibited for any of this my contribution to all the excitement has to be the pictures. I hope they convey some of the enjoyment and pleasure we found in the wonderful things to do and see in New York.

Beryl Cook

BERYL COOK'S
NEW YORK

Breakfast at
The Royalton Hotel

Scrambled eggs and bacon coming up here in the hotel café. The waitress chewed gum and called me honey, just as I'd seen on the films, and the breakfasts were delicious. Bran muffins were my downfall and I see from the Chef's empty tray that he's just delivered new supplies and is going back for more. I hope.

De Cocoa
& Hot Chocolate

We nearly always had a rest in the hotel in the afternoons and watched television whilst getting ready to go out for the evening. Judge Wapner giving his verdicts on the court cases became mesmerising, and an advertisement for removing hair that I particularly liked was of three pairs of women's legs with a man's hand sliding up and down the smooth, silky, unshaven leg of each – no stubble! These two singers appeared in one programme, performing in a night club in Harlem. They were so gorgeous I drew them as they were singing "I Love the Boys", rushing to get in all the details of their clothes.

A Bathroom

We had a most comfortable hotel bedroom, very large, and I took great fancy to the bathroom. I drew this one afternoon whilst lying on the bed and this is what I could see through the doorway. Well, perhaps there weren't four girls in there enjoying a shower together, but the picture was dreadfully dull without them.

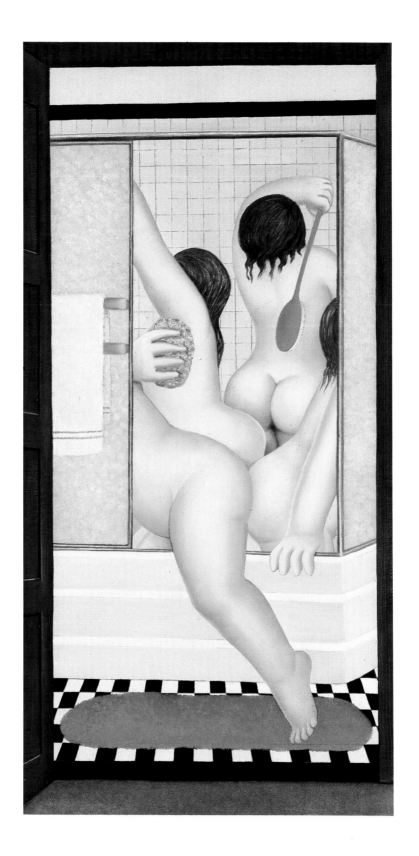

Chicken Suits

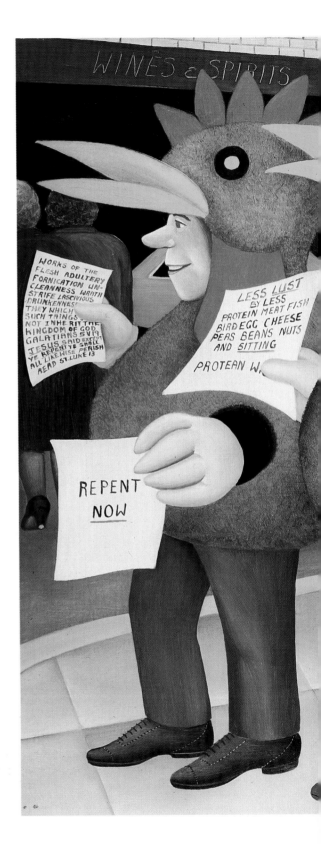

It took ages to amble up to Central Park, with so many distractions in the streets. A man in a mask being filmed, someone riding to work on a monocycle, five being rounded up by the police, a Salvation Army band playing on one corner and on another – these two dressed in fluffy chicken suits handing out leaflets. Being so busy watching, and taking notes, I omitted a very important item – the leaflets they were handing out. The ones I had to use were pressed upon me years ago in London and at last they've come in handy.

Six Thousand
Women Running

*And here are the 3645th, 6th and
7th just passing our seat, under a
shady tree in Central Park. It was
quite exhausting, watching them all
running, and waiting to give a
cheer to the friend who had told us
about it. On a previous visit to the
park we had found ourselves near a
little green dell, surrounded by
trees, in which several men were
sunbathing. This was a most
peaceful scene, quite silent, just
watching eyes, and I thought it
would make a good background for
the race.*

The Park Bench

On the days which promised to be very hot we'd go up into the park to sit for an hour or two, sometimes feeding the squirrels. Until, that is, I heard one little girl warn another that she'd catch both fleas and rabies from them, when they were hastily abandoned by me. This one, and the very handsome park bench, were down by the lake but I brought them up here so I could show some skyscrapers in the distance, and this is my one and only attempt to paint them. I am really only interested in painting figures so have to be very strict and not allow myself to do them until I have painted the background.

Bicyclist

If only it were ME cycling and singing to the music, dressed in a snappy red outfit. Loud rock music announced his arrival and then I saw how attractive his clothes were. It took me some considerable time to draw the bicycle and I gave it up several times, but I liked him so much I persevered. As time went on I found I was dealing with more and more man, less and less bicycle. Which is just as well for I suspect that the wheels would have been too tiny to carry him.

The Museum of Modern Art

A short pause in the cafe here, for a massage of the aching feet and a chocolate brownie. The other lady hurries off for a further session of art appreciation whilst the porter gazes calmly, having seen it all before. I hope you notice the abstract paintings on the wall; I felt I had been rather successful with these, not to mention the rather startling floor, and wonder whether I should go in for them in a big way.

Cocktails for Three

*We left New York in a Greyhound
Bus and some two and a half hours
later arrived at a large hotel in
Atlantic City, where we were each
handed ten dollars in quarters.
Retiring to the bar to discuss the
investment of this unexpected
bonus we found a very attractive
waitress coming down the stairs
with a tray of cocktails. I now think
they could not possibly have been as
lurid as I have painted them,
despite all the careful notes I made.
This isn't where my ten dollars
went though, I lost it all on . . .*

Slot Terrace No. 4

As I made it last for two days I don't think I need ever worry about becoming a compulsive gambler. A greater worry was that I might miss something going on in that exciting atmosphere, with lights flashing, bells ringing and the crash of tokens cascading out of the machines. Crowning it all, for me, was the lift with the transparent wall so that floor upon floor of slot machines were revealed as we swiftly descended. What I couldn't remember was how the lift worked, or landed, and so that I could quickly get on with painting all the hands and arms working the machines, I've shrouded these little details in darkness and a tasteful display of greenery.

Woman with Cigar

*Some people played two machines,
and this little lady also smoked a
cigar to help her concentration.
They were just in front of a bar, and
a waitress told us they seemed to
pay out more when close to bars or
restaurants. I think this could be
true but we hadn't time to test it for
we were off to catch the bus. I
wished I had got one of the cigarette
boxes (or lighters) in the shape of a
slot machine that two men were
examining as they laughed, drank
and discussed their winnings on the
way back to New York.*

Bryant Park

This small park was near our hotel. As it was pretty early in the day I didn't know whether she had spent the night there or was simply taking her ease in the morning sunlight. Nothing much seemed to be going on, just small groups of men talking together, and it was so pleasant that I suggested we get some coffee to drink as we sat there. John said he thought not, better to be moving on, and I learnt later that Bryant Park is not the wisest place to hang about. Especially if you're tourists.

Revolving Door

This started out to be an enormous picture of my most favourite cafe, the Automat. The harder I worked at it the more it became reduced, and in the end I am left only with the revolving door – and the two bag ladies coming through it of course. They had a little heckling session about tokens (for the automat) with a short-tempered assistant in a kiosk, after which they lurched off cackling together to get a cup of coffee. Considering the number of hours we spent in here, and the quantity of photographs we took, I'm very disappointed that I've only been able to produce this small painting.

Bus Ride

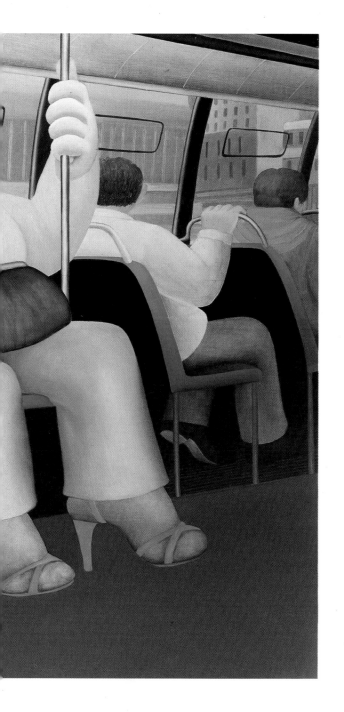

There was lots of laughter and discussion of husbands from these three as they travelled on the bus with us to Chinatown. I guessed from their pretty clothes that they were going out to enjoy themselves, and their legs swung out in rhythm as the bus raced over the bumps in the road and hurtled around corners. I would like to have shown just this, but after every effort on my part, only one pair of legs is swinging.

'To Go'

Sausages, biscuits and gravy in this case, and I hope she enjoys it as much as I did. We found that some restaurants are closed on Sundays, and there are queues outside others, so we staggered up to the hotel bedroom with our arms full of brown paper bags from Bojangles.

Russian Tea Room

One day we had lunch here. When I had finished looking at all the lovely paintings I settled down to eating and to observing all the busy activity around us. I learned that a lot of people have favourite seats, some being especially desirable. Here is the one I have chosen for mine, with some intellectuals enjoying brandy and cigars. I don't very often paint teeth and perhaps in this picture you can see why.

White with Rage

We had intended to go to Coney Island on the day I saw this, but a thick mist made us decide to go instead to Christopher Street with friends. As we sat at a table outside a café, innocently enjoying a cup of tea, a filthy row blew up behind us. She was refusing to pay her bill and the police arrived to sort it out. Furious, she flung the money on the ground and flounced off. I painted her white with rage, and transferred the little group to Brooklyn Heights so I could put them in front of the steps with decorative wrought-iron railings. This move I almost immediately regretted, for in the time it took me to paint the railings I could easily have beaten the iron out myself, by hand.

Hosts & Hostesses

I'm fascinated by shoes, and as we walked into Roseland I found a large showcase full of them. Some were enormous, bigger even than mine. This was reassuring, and we went on into the ballroom and sat near the dance floor. I soon realised that the large table next to ours was for the hosts and hostesses, who charged a dollar a dance. I watched some dance every dance and worried about those not quite so popular. Sometimes they all sat down together and chatted, and this is what I chose for a picture, making a careful arrangement of legs and feet.

Tango

I love dancing of all sorts, not doing it, just watching. These two came to my notice because of the tremendous effort it was for him to raise her again once she'd reached the floor. This became quite worrying – needlessly I think, for they did it many, many times and she was very petite. The man in the bomber jacket was much in demand as a partner and although he had some difficulty with the platform soles he twirled and side-stepped round the floor for every dance.

Rumba

During the rumba all the arms seemed to be flung upwards at the same time, which was very appealing to me for a lot of my paintings are arranged round the hands. I wondered whether it is because most of the dancers had had lessons, and the steps tended to follow the same pattern. I loved Roseland, all the decorations and the happy atmosphere. I wish we had one in Plymouth.

Reading the Newspaper

We took the subway to Coney Island, and found ourselves surrounded by these exotic decorations. This interested me immensely for we had travelled on others with none at all, and until now I had only seen it on television. Sitting near us was this striking businesswoman, reading placidly through the journey regardless of stops, starts and even a youth waving a cup and demanding money. We all ignored him and he departed for a more fruitful carriage.

Coney Island

It was a lovely sunny day at Coney Island, and not many people about as it was before the season had started. We bought a plastic Mickey Mouse and Miss Piggy, then some lunch and sat on a seat on the boardwalk. There was only one family on the miles and miles of beach and whilst they sat in the sunshine father exercised, running on the spot, jumping and leaping continuously. I craftily painted in two footprints, to show he is jumping and not just hanging about in mid-air.

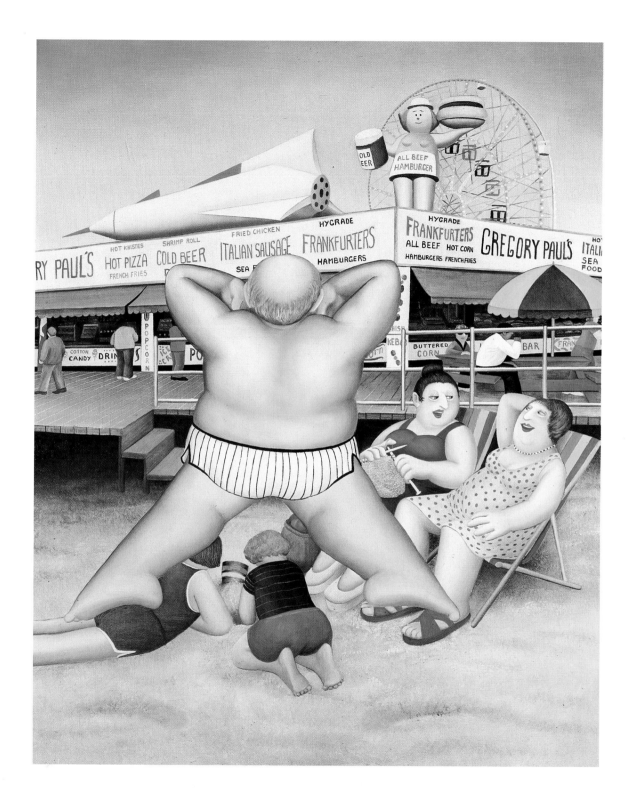

Rye over Rocks

We often went into Grand Central Station, visiting all the bars in turn, and one evening, before dining on oysters there, I saw this lady waiting to catch a train. She ordered rye over rocks (twice) and this must have been greatly needed after a day's shopping. We were served by a pretty waitress in very skimpy clothing, and most of her is squeezed in at the top of the picture. Do you notice the expert rendering of the 'rocks'? I had one myself after painting them.

Botanical Gardens

We caught a train and, getting off too early, we had a long walk through the Bronx until we were joined by a regular visitor to the gardens who showed us the way. He told us he went there every day, to sit and listen to his wireless. Large groups of children were arriving in yellow school buses, and we all went round admiring the sights and views together. Well, not all of us were admiring the sights and views, some were fighting and arguing. I had noticed these little girls on a tube train, and thought it would be a good opportunity for me to show their attractive, intricately woven, hairstyles.

Street Market

*Time flies by in the street markets
near Canal Street, so does money.
Most of the treasures we had to
leave behind on the stalls I'm sorry
to say. There were lots of little
look-alike dogs, half poodle, half
pekingese and half terrier. Now this
is not easy to depict, as I found
when I came to paint them, and the
more paint I added the messier they
became. The man in the big hat was
very tall and good-looking. He was
outside the station when I saw him,
but I thought he'd just fit in here.*

Lunch in the
Gardens

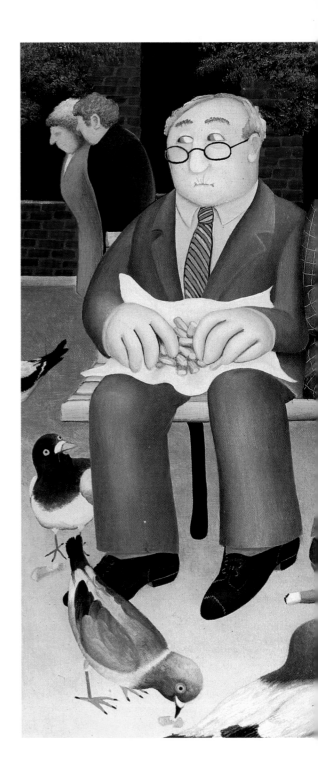

Fortunately there are lots of shady places to sit between bouts of bargain hunting. I think these four were probably from an office nearby, enjoying their lunch in the fresh air. Not exactly gourmet, but very pleasant and much appreciated by the pigeons.

Bar and Barbara

The Algonquin was opposite our hotel on 44th Street and each time we passed it I mingled with the people going in and out, hoping to hear some witty conversation. Expectations rose further when we were invited to tea there one afternoon by a journalist acquaintance, but after finding that we were not sitting at a big round table – only a small square one – all our attention was directed to the sandwiches and cakes. I was discussing this with two friends recently, who were talking about their forthcoming trip to New York, and I grew more and more excited as they described the fur coats they'd be wearing and the parts of Manhattan they would be visiting. So much so that I transposed them to this location, one in Persian Lamb and one in Sable, before they had even left these shores. Now I accuse them of spending all their holiday drinking cocktails in the Algonquin, which they hotly deny.

Nathans

I watched a little tiny man high up in the sky painting an advertisement on a huge hoarding over Nathans on Broadway one morning, and wondered what it felt like to be up there. I decided that I too would paint a hoarding for New York and here it is, with me painting it. I don't know why I chose Adam and Eve, but the background is from a photograph taken inside the conservatory at the Botanical Gardens. Adam looks rather doubtful, could it be at the size of the apple? The hardest work here was in making the strategic placement of arms, mine and Eve's, so I didn't have to get too personal.

Design by Ian Craig
Photography by Rodney Todd-White & Co

Beryl Cook's Paintings are sold in London
through Portal Gallery Ltd

Limited edition prints are available from The
Alexander Gallery, Bristol

Greetings cards are published by Gallery Five
Ltd, London